100

things you should know about

WORLD
WONDERS

100

things you should know about

WORLD
WONDERS

Adam Hibbert

Consultant: Philip Steele

BARNES & NOBLE

NEW YORK

Barnes & Noble Publishing, Inc.
122 Fifth Avenue
New York, NY 10011

ISBN-13: 978-0-7607-5965-3
ISBN-10: 0-7607-5965-0

Printed and bound in China

06 07 08 09 MCH 10 9 8 7 6 5 4 3 2

Library of Congress Cataloging-in-Publication Data available upon request.

Editorial Director: Belinda Gallagher
Art Director: Jo Brewer
Editorial Assistant: Bethanie Bourne
Volume Designer: John Christopher, White Design
Copy Editor: Sarah Ridley
Proofreader: Hayley Kerr
Indexer: Jane Parker

ACKNOWLEDGEMENTS
The publishers would like to thank the following artists who
have contributed to this book:

Lisa Alderson
Syd Brak
Kuo Kang Chen
Peter Dennis
Richard Draper
Nicholas Forder
Mike Foster/Maltings Partnership
Luigi Galante
Alan Hancock

John James
Alessandro Menchi
Kevin Maddison
Janos Marffy
Terry Riley
Martin Sanders
Rudi Vizi
Steve Weston
John Woodcock

Cartoons by Mark Davis at Mackerel

Contents

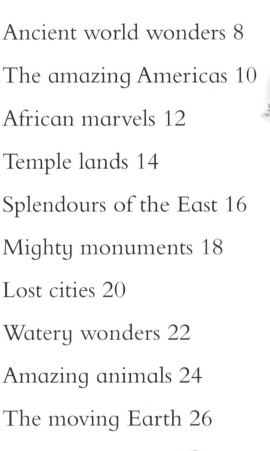

Wonder of Greece

1 **A goddess once lived in a temple in Greece.** The Parthenon was a temple built to honor the goddess Athena. It is still one of the best examples of ancient Greek architecture. The temple was built from beautiful white marble. It contained a vast sculpture of the goddess Athena, which would have amazed and terrified visitors. Remains of the temple still stand today on the Acropolis, a hill overlooking the city of Athens.

▶ The temple complex at the Acropolis was dotted with statues and smaller temples, as well as housing the main temple, the Parthenon. Inside the Parthenon was a sculpture of Athena over 40 feet (12 meters) tall, made of gold and ivory.

Parthenon, home of Athena

Ancient world wonders

2 **The Romans built a massive stadium for deadly duels.** The Colosseum was a giant stone stadium that held crowds of 50,000 people. Emperors and other rich Romans paid for "games" including gladiator battles and prisoner fights with wild beasts. The arena could be flooded for miniature naval battles between gladiator armies.

3 **The great lighthouse at Alexandria, Egypt, was more than 320 feet (100 meters) tall, with a blazing fire at the top.** It stood for 1,500 years until it was destroyed by an earthquake. The lighthouse was built during the reign of pharaoh Ptolemy II (283–246BC) and became known as one of the seven wonders of the ancient world.

▼ The Colosseum was opened by the emperor Titus in AD80. It was so well designed that huge crowds could get in and out of the building in minutes.

Less wealthy people had to sit further away from the main arena

Masts could hold a canvas roof to protect spectators from the heat of the sun

Arches supported the weight of the seating

The main arena was covered in sand

The building was decorated with beautiful statues

◄ The Great Sphinx was carved from stone over 4,500 years ago.

6 The ancient Greek Temple of Artemis was hidden under a swamp.

The archaeologist John Wood discovered it in the 19th century. The temple was built over the site of two earlier shrines at Ephesus, Asia Minor. It was dedicated to the goddess Artemis. Archaeologists are still finding the offerings of pilgrims from across the Greek world.

4 A giant man–lion protects the pyramids.

The Great Sphinx is a huge statue of a half-man, half-lion that guards the pyramids at Giza, Egypt. It probably shows the dead king Khafre as a man with the fearsome power of a lion. The Sphinx is so old that sand blowing in the wind has rubbed away detail of the lion's body and parts of Khafre's face.

▲ The Temple of Artemis was famous for its beautiful marble decoration.

5 The Hanging Gardens didn't really hang.

Greeks were amazed by the city of Babylon, in modern Iraq. They found a fantastic garden with terraces on different levels, covered by spectacular plants. It was said that a Babylonian king had it built to remind his queen, who was from a mountain region, of her childhood.

▶ To water The Hanging Gardens, slaves worked in shifts, lifting water from the Euphrates River.

7 Alexandria's famous library was burnt to cinders.

Arts, math and sciences were developed more in Alexandria, Egypt, than anywhere else in the ancient world. Most of the knowledge recorded in the library was lost when Christians burnt it to the ground in the year AD391.

The amazing Americas

◄ The mountain city of Machu Picchu was a forgotten marvel, lost for 400 years.

8 The Egyptians weren't the only ones to build pyramids. Some pyramid-builders lived in Central and South America. Instead of using them as tombs, the Incas, the Maya and the Aztecs used their pyramids as temples. Without modern technology, a pyramid shape is the safest one to use for big buildings.

9 The Incas built a mountaintop city. Machu Picchu was a city high in the Andes Mountains, with gardens, a temple, and a fortress. The city was built from large, interlocking stones and watered by a spring at the top of the mountain. It was so well-hidden, Spanish invaders never found it. In 1911, the city was rediscovered by American explorer Hiram Bingham.

10 Not all monuments are built of stone. The Nazca people scratched huge patterns and pictures into the stony deserts of Peru, which are only properly visible from the air. Some of the patterns are simple squares and triangles, and some are line drawings of animals, such as a spider and a monkey. No one knows for certain what they were for.

11 **Chan Chan was an amazing city built of mud bricks (adobe).** The Chimú were farming people who became wealthy and created a small empire in Peru. The richest Chimú families built compounds in Chan Chan. Each compound contained gardens, pyramids, and warehouses. They were decorated with beautiful carvings and patterns.

12 **Teotihuacán was the greatest city in the New World.** Before Europeans arrived in the Americas, this civilization rose and fell in Mexico. It left a huge city, with two great pyramids dedicated to the Sun and Moon, and a vast temple for Quetzalcóatl, the feathered snake god.

▼ The Moon Pyramid of Teotihuacán contains the remains of six smaller buildings.

I DON'T BELIEVE IT!

Spanish explorers searched for a mystery city they called El Dorado— where everything was supposed to be made of gold.

13 **The Aztecs farmed on a lake.** After the Aztecs founded their capital city on an island in a lake, their society began to grow. They made the island bigger by building flat platforms of reed and coating them with mud from the lake bottom. Then they grew crops and raised animals on the platforms.

African marvels

14 **Nigeria was a center of metalwork wonders.** The Benin Empire was founded in the 11th century AD. It was famous for its brass sculptures. Benin City, the capital, survived until 1897, when the British destroyed it, taking thousands of statues.

◀ The brass sculptures of Benin, such as this head, were produced from the 1500s onward.

15 **In Cameroon, the pyramids were made from bamboo.** Many different Africans came to the Bamileke region to settle. Some built the pyramid roofs of their houses out of long bamboo stalks, then hoisted them into the air and placed the walls underneath. They were up to 33 feet (10 meters) tall.

16 **Zimbabwe was a great stone city.** All through the Middle Ages, a powerful African nation had its center at Great Zimbabwe. Around a fortified stone compound with its impressive tower, the stone buildings covered the valley and a nearby hilltop. The Karanga people used the local gold to trade with partners as far away as China.

◀ Around this stone compound in Zimbabwe, the House of the Great Woman, rose a great city of 20,000 Africans.

17

Mali's mosque looks like a giant sandcastle. Djenne is home to an amazing mosque. It is built by hand from mud and mud bricks, with wooden steps poking through the surface to help builders scramble up and down. Djenne was once an important trading post and center of Muslim thought. The mosque is repaired with fresh mud each spring, in a huge festival involving the whole community.

▼ The Great Mosque of Djenne is 100 years old. It stands where great mosques have stood for 800 years.

18

St. George's Church in Ethiopia is made from one solid rock. In about AD1200, King Lalibela started a programme of church-building. The builders dug a deep trench around a massive rock, carved it into the shape of a cross, and then hollowed it out to make the church.

19

Dogon houses were shaped like people. The Dogon tribe of Mali built their houses to represent a person lying on the floor—with a fireplace for a head, store rooms for arms, a workroom for the belly, and stables in the place of legs.

AFRICAN QUIZ

1. The Benin Empire was famous for (a) wooden carvings or (b) brass sculptures?
2. Pyramids in Cameroon were built with (a) bamboo or (b) grass?
3. The Karanga people traded with (a) gold or (b) silver?
4. The Great Mosque of Djenne is (a) 50 years or (b) 100 years old?

Answers:
1b 2a 3a 4b

13

Temple lands

20 **King Kashyapa ruled from inside a lion.** The Sri Lankan king's mountain fortress was known as Sigiriya, or Lion's Mouth, because it could only be reached by climbing through gates carved in the shape of a lion's gaping jaw. His fortress was on a small plateau, 600 feet (180 meters) above the plain below.

▲ The Lion's Mouth gate to Sigiriya has gone, but the two giant lion's paws remain.

21 **The city of Pagan had 4,000 Buddhist shrines.** Pagan was once the capital of Burma (modern-day Myanmar) in Southeast Asia. In the city's richest era, from around 1060 to 1280, thousands of Buddhist shrines and monuments were built. The city has since disappeared, but 2,000 shrines can still be seen.

22 **Khajraho's 85 temples were lost for 500 years.** India's Chandela kings abandoned their Hindu temple city of Khajraho for the safety of hill forts during a chaotic period of India's history. Later Muslim rulers knew nothing of the Hindu shrines, so they survived unharmed until they were rediscovered in 1838 by a British army officer.

I DON'T BELIEVE IT!

We still can't crack the code of writings on 4000-year-old tablets from the Harappa Empire in India.

24
A temple in Java swallowed a hill! Buddhists built one huge shrine at Borobudur, by shaping a small hill and casing it with stone blocks. They added some amazing sculpture. Since 1972 all 800,000 stones have been taken away, cleaned, and replaced.

◄ The Borobudur "hill" temple of Java is home to 2,000 carvings, 72 shrines, and 500 Buddhas.

23
Farmers built staircases on mountains. Water-loving rice plants can't grow on steep hills, but East Asian farmers found ways to use their mountain landscape. They made stepped terraces that could hold muddy pools for their crops. Whole mountains were transformed.

▼ The moat around Angkor Wat measures 20 mi (6 km). It is as wide as three jumbo jets.

25
Angkor Wat was the biggest temple ever built. The Khmer kingdom in Cambodia was believed to be ruled by god-kings. Their capital at Angkor contained a huge complex of temple buildings, with artificial lakes, moats, and long boundary walls covered in carvings. The biggest temple, Angkor Wat, was saved from the jungle by Buddhist monks after the Khmer kingdom collapsed.

Splendors of the East

26 One wall is 3,800 miles (6,400 kilometers) long. Chinese civilization was based on farming, and the early Chinese nation was often raided by nomads from the North. From 214BC, China built a wall to keep its neighbours out. The wall was 30 feet (9 meters) high, with watchtowers and a walkway along the top for the guards.

▲ The Great Wall of China includes many walls built by different emperors over several centuries. The Wall was originally dotted with watchtowers.

▼ Thousands of clay soldiers were buried with Emperor Qin Shi Huangdi to make him mighty in heaven.

27 There is a city inside the city of Beijing. The emperor of China once lived inside his own city, with hundreds of buildings and 9,000 rooms, all contained within 10 miles (16 kilometers) of high walls. It was known as the Forbidden City because no one was allowed to enter without an invitation from the emperor's court. It is now a museum.

28 An emperor was buried with clay soldiers. According to Chinese tradition, the dead should be buried or cremated with items that would be useful to them in heaven. Normally this means a few handfuls of money. But the first emperor of China, Qin Shi Huangdi, was buried with 7,000 life-size clay soldiers.

29

Japanese tombs were shaped like keyholes. Japan became a powerful country in the Yamato era, between AD250 and 500. The Yamato nobles were buried in huge tombs, which are keyhole-shaped when seen from above. It took 800,000 people to build Emperor Nintoku's tomb.

30

A giant Buddha sits in the world's biggest wooden building. The Todai-ji Temple in Japan is 188 feet (57 meters) long, 165 feet (50 meters) wide and 154 feet (47 meters) high, but used to be even bigger. For almost 1,500 years it has been the home of a giant Buddha made from 130 tons of bronze and leafed in 285 pounds (130 kilograms) of gold.

▶ The Todai-ji Buddha promises peace after conflict. Each finger is over 3 feet (one meter) long.

31

Koreans were early astronomers. The ancient Silla kingdom of Korea was ruled by Queen Sondok, in the 7th century. She had an observatory built for studying the stars. The observatory still stands today, although it is not used.

Mighty monuments

32 **Stone giants on Easter Island weigh as much as 1,000 men.** Giant stone statues, called *moai*, frightened the first European visitors to Easter Island in the Pacific Ocean. The biggest of the 600 figures weighs at least 75 tons, not including its 11-ton hat, called a *pukao*. Carved from single blocks of stone, the statues were moved great distances before being placed to mark tombs. The eyes were made of coral.

◄ The mysterious giant heads on Easter Island have frightened sailors for hundreds of years.

33 **Ancient Britons built a huge stone circle.** Stonehenge in England was made from giant stones, some of which were brought 230 miles (385 kilometers) from a quarry in Wales. They were arranged so that the sun shined into the entranceway on the morning of the longest day of summer—the summer solstice. The solstice was the most important festival day for farmers. People prayed that crops would grow well before harvesting.

► Stonehenge was built 4,000 years ago.

34
One giant mound in Britain is a total mystery. The same ancient Britons who built Stonehenge also built Silbury Hill near Avebury, another stone circle. Its purpose is unknown. It is 130 feet (40 meters) tall and 100 feet (30 meters) across at the top. There is no sign of a tomb inside.

35
Some religious parades may have lasted half a mile or more. Holy men of northern France may have walked the long, stone avenue at Carnac, Brittany, every sunrise and sunset. Prehistoric religious carvings on some of the stones there were later added to with Roman graffiti and Christian symbols.

STONE CRAZY!
Large stone structures built by prehistoric people are called megaliths. The people who made them had no metal tools. Some megaliths were carved from blocks of stone using handheld stone chisels. But to carve stone with a stone, you have to know which stone is toughest. Try placing these stones in order of hardness:

a. Marble b. Granite
c. Diamond d. Limestone
e. Quartz

Answers: c e b a d

36
Temples on the island of Malta have stood for 5,000 years. The oldest buildings in the world are in Malta. Ancient farmers worshiped goddesses of fertility and built temples out of limestone for religious rituals. The temples housed small statues of an "earth mother" goddess.

Lost cities

37 **Ancient cities have been swallowed by the sea.** The sea level in the Mediterranean has changed since cities began to be built around it. The coastline of Lebanon is dotted with underwater cities, such as Yarmuta, which were abandoned as the sea rose. The Black Sea coastline was pushed back at a speed of more than half a mile a day when the Mediterranean began to pour in, 7,500 years ago.

▲ According to legend, the island of Atlantis sunk beneath the sea. Scientists now think that stories about Atlantis could relate to the Greek island of Thira, which was destroyed by volcanic eruptions in 1470BC.

38 **The island of Atlantis was lost in legend.** The ancient Greeks told stories of an island in the Atlantic Ocean that once sent armies to rule the Mediterranean. But legend has it that the island sank below the waves after earthquake damage.

I DON'T BELIEVE IT!

There are three Roman columns near Naples in Italy that have been nibbled by shellfish. This proves they were underwater at some point. Volcanic activity can push or drop the coastline by several yards.

39 **Cleopatra's palace lies below fishing boats.** After the Romans took over Alexandria in Egypt around 100BC, the city became less important. Alexandrians moved their city inland, away from the rising sea. The old city is now being found under the waters of the harbor.

40 An Egyptian city appeared in America. A huge Egyptian sphinx was uncovered not far from El Paso, Texas, in 1999. But it turned out not to be real. It was a set for a film, *The Ten Commandments*. It had been hidden by Cecil B. de Mille in 1923 to keep details of the film secret before it was released.

41 There may be a city deep beneath the ocean near Cuba. Scientists have scanned the seabed of an area, Cabo de San Antonio, off the coast of Cuba. They have seen regular-shaped structures 2,000 feet (600 meters) down, but cannot tell if the street and house shapes are man-made or something natural, such as coral.

42 Japan's undersea pyramid may be a freak of nature. Off the southernmost island of Japan, close to Taiwan, a stone mound has been discovered by divers, with what could be steps, carvings and a roadway. It looks like an Inca temple, but geologists say that all the odd features could be explained by the effect of waves smashing into the rock.

▲ This underwater "pyramid" off the coast of Yonaguni Island, Japan, could be the oldest man-made structure ever found.

Watery wonders

43 Undersea vents feed spooky creatures. Almost all life on Earth depends on the Sun to provide energy. But undersea vents feed some very strange-looking life forms. They give off clouds of hot water that contain minerals. These feed tiny plants and animals, which are eaten by tube worms and giant clams, a kind of shellfish.

44 The deepest place in the sea is the Mariana Trench. It marks the spot where the huge Pacific plate plunges beneath the continental plate of East Asia. It is 1,500 miles (2,500 kilometers) long, and some parts are over 7 miles (11 kilometers) below sea level.

Rat tail fish

Giant clams

I DON'T BELIEVE IT!

Before ships had engines, the oceans were a quieter place for animals to live. Whales could hear their mates calling from the other side of the world!

Cloud of hot water rich in minerals

Rocky chimney made from a build up of minerals

45

There's a mountain range under the Atlantic Ocean. The mountain chain is 10,000 miles (16,000 kilometers) long and lies halfway between the Americas on one side, and Europe and Africa on the other. The seabed is growing from volcanic rock, forcing the two sides of the Atlantic apart at a rate of up to 4 inches (10 centimeters) a year. As the seabed is pressed, it crumples into mountains.

46

North America was hit by a wave 1,600 feet (488 meters) tall. In Lituya Bay, Alaska, trees were smashed from the bay by a record-breaking wave in 1958. Scientists think it was caused by a piece of a mountain crashing into the head of the bay. The wave reached 1,700 feet (520 meters) above sea level.

◀ An amazing variety of life thrives in the deep ocean near hot underwater vents.

Tube worms

Amazing animals

47 A monarch butterfly flies 1,800 miles (3,000 kilometers). Monarch butterflies in North America swarm together for a winter vacation. They fly from colder northern areas down to the forests of southern California and Mexico. In spring they return some of the way, lay eggs and die. Their young continue the trip north for summer.

▲ Monarch butterflies live in several parts of the world, but the American species travels furthest.

48 On Christmas Island in the Indian Ocean, the ground turns red twice a year. Red forest-living crabs migrate in huge swarms to the seashore, where their eggs are laid all at once. Then their tiny young return after a few months as larvae.

▲ Red crabs have to dip in the ocean after their long walk, to save themselves from drying out.

▶ This coral polyp has built itself a cup of limestone, making a shelter like a snail's shell.

49 Tiny corals build a home you can see from space.

The Great Barrier Reef runs up the northeast coast of Australia for 1,200 miles (2,000 kilometers). It is built by billions of tiny coral polyps, less than half an inch across. Over a period of 20 million years, these tiny animals have created a world wonder that can be seen from space.

coral polyp

50 Termite cities have air conditioning.

Termite nests are often out of sight, but some poke up through the soil to form strange mounds. In northern Australia, these nests line up north to south. Scientists think the termites use the Sun's energy to circulate cool air within the nest.

▶ Termite mounds are built to keep the right mix of air and moisture in the nest below.

I DON'T BELIEVE IT!

Sea creatures often produce millions of eggs, because so many will be eaten by hungry predators.

The moving Earth

51 The rocks at the bottom of the Grand Canyon are two billion years old. The Colorado River has worn away tons of rock, creating a canyon that runs for 278 miles (446 kilometers). In places, the canyon is one mile (1.6 kilometers) deep and 18 miles (29 kilometers) wide.

52 A meteorite left a hole in Arizona. Barringer Crater in the United States is half a mile across and 600 feet (180 meters) deep. Droplets of metal and glass can be found for up to 60 miles (100 kilometers) around the crater. They are the remains of a metal meteorite, which exploded on impact with Earth.

▼ A 300,000-ton metal meteorite crashed into Arizona and exploded about 50,000 years ago. It left this enormous crater in the earth.

53 The wind can make a mountain of sand. The Dune of Pilat on the French Atlantic coast has been created by wind and waves piling up sand from the bay over the last 200 years. The dune is 345 feet (105 meters) high, 1,640 feet (500 meters) wide and nearly 2 miles (3 kilometers) long. It is slowly creeping inland. A pine forest has been planted to try to slow it down.

55 **Africa is tearing apart along the Rift Valley.** This giant tear— 2,500 miles (4,000 kilometers) long, 60 miles (100 kilometers) wide and up to 12 miles (2 kilometers) deep, is forming as Africa and Asia slowly pull apart. The tear has allowed hot rock from below to force through in places, forming mountains such as Mount Kilimanjaro.

I DON'T BELIEVE IT!

Before it was dammed, the Colorado River carried 500,000 tons of sand and sediment a day—enough grit to cut through the toughest rock.

▼ It can take rock climbers four days to climb El Capitan.

54 **Yosemite was carved by tons of ice.** The Yosemite National Park, in the Sierra Nevada, United States, has some of the most amazing rocks in the world. El Capitan is a smooth block of granite rising half a mile from the valley below. It was carved out of the landscape by a huge glacier that slid past like a giant sheet of sandpaper.

Outrageous rock!

56 **The rock of Uluru changes color through the day.** The weird lump of rock lying stranded in Australia's outback is a sacred site for Aborigines. Once known as Ayers Rock, the reddish sandstone goes through amazing color changes at sunrise and sunset. Grooves and holes worn by rain and sandstorms create a strange series of shadows that move across the stone.

57 **Rock can make a bridge.** American Indians believed that a rainbow had been turned to stone when they visited the Rainbow Bridge, 305 feet (93 meters) high and 275 feet (85 meters) long, in Utah. The sandstone bridge can appear pink, red, or lavender-colored in sunlight.

▶ A walk around the base of Uluru covers almost 6 miles (10 kilometers). The rock has lots of small caves, of which many are covered with Aboriginal paintings.

58 Huge rooms can be carved from rock. The caves at Sarawak, Malaysia, are gigantic. The Deer Cave is almost 330 feet (100 meters) wide, 330 feet (100 meters) high, and over 1 mile 2 km) long! That's enough room for 20 football fields.

59 Some rocks used to be trees. Near Winslow, Arizona, the desert is covered with stone logs—fossils of giant trees that once grew there. The logs crystallized as they lay in mud, and were buried for millions of years. The crystals preserve details such as the growth rings of the tree trunks.

I DON'T BELIEVE IT!

There is a desert of white sand in New Mexico. The grains of sand are made from gypsum. Rare white lizards and mice have evolved to blend in with the white background.

Hot stuff!

60 Volcanoes can make neat sidewalks. The Giant's Causeway in Ireland was formed by a volcano's lava flow. It cooled slowly, cracking from the surface downward like drying mud, to form six-sided stone "logs." Irish tradition says that it was built by a giant who wanted to make a road to Scotland.

▼ Some of the stone columns of Giant's Causeway are up to 20 feet (6 meters) high.

61 The Earth can spit boiling water. Wherever heat from below ground makes contact with water, you can find hot springs and geysers. Whakarewarewa is New Zealand's most spectacular hot spring area. Bubbling mud and hot springs are overshadowed by Pohutu, a geyser that hurls water and steam 100 feet (30 meters) into the air.

MAKE A GEYSER

You can create a safe geyser by releasing all the bubbles in a bottle of fizzy water at once. Standing outside, give the bottle a vigorous shake and undo the cap. There she blows!

63

When volcanoes die, they can leave houses behind. The Urgup Cones in Turkey are all that is left of small volcanoes. Their outer layers have worn away, exposing solid lava cones that once filled the volcanoes' inner chambers. They have been carved out to make houses.

64

You can enjoy a concert in a lava bubble. As lava flows from a volcano, it cools from the outside, forming hard rock while the centre remains liquid. Sometimes this leaves a cave or tube inside the rock. At Cueva de los Verdes, in the Canary Islands, caves like these have been converted to make a concert hall.

▲ Houses carved from the Urgup Cones can be cool in summer and warm in winter.

▼ Mount Fuji is a volcano, which last erupted in 1707. It is visible from Tokyo, over 60 miles (100 kilometers) away.

62

Pilgrims visit the volcano of Fuji. Mount Fuji is Japan's biggest mountain—the result of thousands of eruptions of ash and lava. The shrines that circle the lip of the volcano's crater are home to young trainee priests in the Shinto religion.

Fantastic lakes

65 **Lakes can be found in the strangest places.** Crater Lake in Oregon is a beautiful, crystal-blue color, but it's at the top of a mountain. When the old volcano, Mount Mazama, last erupted it left a bowl-shaped crater 6 miles (10 kilometers) across and almost 2,000 feet (600 meters) deep. Water from melted ice and snow has filled the bowl.

66 **You can visit an island on a lake on an island on a lake.** Lake Huron in North America has a large island, Manitoulin Island, the biggest island in any lake in the world. On Manitoulin is Lake Manitou, which is also big and has several smaller islands in it.

▼ The United States's deepest lake, Crater Lake, has a small volcano called Wizard Island in the middle. The lake is 1,932 feet (589 meters) at its greatest depth.

▶ There is so much salt in the water of the Dead Sea you can easily float.

67 **Some lakes are saltier than the ocean.** The Dead Sea is a lake in the Middle East that is 1,312 feet (400 meters) below sea level. Water quickly evaporates from the lake's surface due to the hot climate, leaving behind minerals such as salt. The Dead Sea is about ten times saltier than seawater.

68 **There's a lake as old as the dinosaurs.** Lake Vostok, near the South Pole, has been cut off from the rest of the world for millions of years under a layer of ice. Scientists are working out how to drill 25 miles (4 kilometers) down to the lake under the ice, without disturbing any life that may survive there.

69 **Lakes can be hidden away completely.** There is a lake in northeastern Namibia, Africa, which is deep underground inside its own cave. Dragon's Breath Cave supports life. With no sunlight, all the cave creatures rely on bat droppings as an energy source. As there is no light, the eyesight of the animals and fish that live there is extremely poor, and other senses such as touch and smell have become more developed.

I DON'T BELIEVE IT!

Lake Baikal in Russia is home to the world's only freshwater seals.

Wonderful waterfalls

70 Niagara Falls is moving upriver. The flowing water eats away at the rock below it, causing the lip of the falls to collapse. The waterfall then moves back a few yards. Niagara has moved about 3 feet (one meter) a year for the last 300 years. It has stabilized now because the Niagara River is redirected at night to hydroelectric power stations. Here, the water is used to provide electricity.

▲ Niagara Falls was formed about 12,000 years ago when a great ice sheet melted, causing the Niagara River to overflow. The Falls form part of the border between The United States and Canada.

71 One waterfall is nearly half a mile tall. Hidden away in the Venezuelan rainforest is a mountain with steep cliffs. The Angel Falls flows over the edge of one of these cliffs, and drops 3,212 feet (979 meters) through the air to the river below. It is the tallest waterfall in the world.

◄ Angel Falls is 15 times taller than Niagara Falls. It was discovered in 1933 by American, Jimmy Angel.

WATERFALL QUIZ
1. How far has Niagara Falls been moving back each year?
2. Where are the Iguaçu Falls?
3. How much taller is Angel Falls than Niagara Falls?

Answers:
1.One yard a year 2. Argentina 3. 15 times taller

▼ The Iguaçu Falls form part of the border between Argentina and Brazil.

72 The Iguaçu waterfall in Argentina makes beautiful rainbows. About 260,000 gallons (12,750 cubic meters) of water pour over the lip of the Falls every second. The waterfall is broken into separate flows by rocky outcrops along the lip, which is 2.5 miles (4 kilometers) long. It creates so much spray that there are often several rainbows at once.

Waterworks!

73 **The Akosombo Dam has made a lake bigger than a country.** Lake Volta is 3,089 square miles (8,000 square kilometers), about three times bigger than the country of Luxembourg. The lake was created by damming the Volta River in 1965 to provide water for arming. The artificial lake is more than a reservoir. It also supplies Ghana with electricity, an inland fishing resource and a navigation system—giving shipping links between the northern end of the country and the coast.

WATERWORKS QUIZ

1. What river was dammed to make the Akosombo Dam?
2. Which canal links two oceans?
3. How long is the Suez Canal?
4. Where is the world's busiest port?
5. Where might you find a lock on a canal?

Answers:
1. Volta River 2. The Panama Canal
3. 60 miles (100 kilometers)
4. Rotterdam 5. Where a canal goes uphill or downhill

▼ The Akosombo Dam was built in the 1960s. Electricity made here supplies three countries and powers Ghana's industries, such as an aluminum factory.

74
One canal links two oceans.
The Panama Canal in Central America connects the Atlantic and Pacific Oceans. It was built to save ships a long detour. At just 40 miles (65 kilometers) long, it saves ships traveling from one side of the United States to the other—a 7,500 mile (12,000-kilometer) trip around South America.

75
You can ride a ship through a desert. In 1869 a French company completed 11 years of engineering to create the 60 mile (100 kilometers) -long Suez Canal. It passes through Egypt, linking the Mediterranean Sea with the Red Sea. The Suez Canal saves ships a 4,785 mile (7,700 kilometers) detour.

Mediterranean Sea

Suez Canal (blue)

Red Sea

▲ The Suez Canal was opened in 1869.

▲ Ships mainly travel through the Suez Canal in single line traffic as the canal is quite narrow.

76
The Dutch can shut a door to stop the tide coming in. Rotterdam is the world's busiest port. It is built on land reclaimed from the Rhine River, and used to be at risk from storm surges in the North Sea. It now has two huge doors that can be shut against high tides. Each door is about 1,000 feet (300 meters) in height—taller than the Eiffel Tower.

77
Some boats use lifts!
When a canal climbs a hill, locks are needed to raise or lower boats, one "step" at a time. This is slow work on a big hill. Instead of a series of locks, some canals have a boat "elevator," which carries a section of the canal, complete with water and boat, from the bottom to the top, or back again.

Shaping our world

▼ Two large fishing ports on the Aral Sea have been left dry as the shoreline drew back.

78 **The Aral Sea is shrinking.**
A huge lake in central Asia called
the Aral Sea was once 50 feet (15 meters)
deeper and twice as big. Rivers supplying it
were used to water fields instead. The Aral Sea
began to shrink and became three times saltier than
it had been before, killing all its fish. Islands across
the middle of the Aral Sea have now joined up,
breaking the water into two separate lakes.

79

Lava can be used to make an island bigger. Iceland sits on the mid-Atlantic volcanic ridge, where there is lots of volcanic activity. In 1973, the villagers on the island of Vestmannaeyjar, Iceland, fought off a lava flow by pumping sea water at it, diverting it into the ocean. The lava formed a new harbor wall for their fishing port, and added 0.8 square miles (2 square kilometers) to their island.

▲ The 1973 lava flow improved the shape of the harbor, giving better shelter to boats.

80

Some countries keep growing bigger. The Netherlands is one of the Low Countries of Europe. They are called "low" because much of their coastal land is actually below sea level. A quarter of the Netherlands has been reclaimed from river estuaries and the ocean by building a system of soil walls, and pumping out the water.

UPHILL FLOW!

If the Low Countries had no way to pump water out, they would soon flood again. Make this simple pump. Ask an adult to help you

You will need:

two plastic bowls   water   plastic tubing   chair

1. Place an empty bowl on the floor.
2. Place a bowl of water on a chair.
3. Put one end of the tube in the bowl of water.
4. Suck through the tube to start the water moving.
5. Place the other end of the tube in the empty bowl. Water will rise up the tube and start to flow into the empty bowl.

81

It took 14 years to carve a mountain. Mount Rushmore in South Dakota, was sculpted by 400 people over 14 years to create four huge stone portraits of American leaders. The side of the mountain that receives most sunlight shows the four faces, each with eyes 13 feet (4 meters) across.

From A to B

82 **Akashi Kaikyo Bridge reaches 1.2 miles (2 kilometers) in one step.** Japan is made up of four big islands and hundreds of smaller ones. People used to have to catch a ferry to travel from one big island, Shikoku, to the main island, Honshu. The Akashi Kaikyo Bridge reaches across the 1.2 miles (2 kilometers) of ocean separating the two islands, allowing people to travel easily and quickly. This is the longest span of a bridge anywhere in the world.

I DON'T BELIEVE IT!

Scotland's Forth Bridge is always being painted. It takes painters three years to paint its 1,710 foot (521 meters) length. By the time they've finished they have to start again.

83 **The longest pilgrimage of all is the Hajj.** For six days in the Islamic calendar's last month of the year, Mecca is host to two million pilgrims. Muslims from all countries and backgrounds come together to walk around the Kaaba in Mecca's Great Mosque, Muslims' holiest point on Earth. They also perform religious ceremonies.

84
Trains zoom at 100 miles (150 kilometers) an hour under the sea. The Eurotunnel connects mainland Britain with northern France. The three tunnels—two railroads and a service tunnel—run under the ocean, as well as under solid ground. Trains carry foot passengers as well as motorists in their own cars.

▲ The Eurotunnel linking Britain and France was first discussed in the 1700s—it was finished in 1995.

85
Sydney Harbour Bridge in Australia is the widest bridge in the world. The bridge, completed in 1932, is almost 165 feet (50 meters) wide—carrying railroad lines, traffic lanes, a bike lane and a footpath.

◀ The Akashi Kaikyo Bridge uses enough cable to circle the Earth seven times.

▲ About 160,000 vehicles cross Sydney Harbour Bridge each day.

Super playgrounds!

86 **The Skydome sports stadium in Toronto, Canada, is one of the world's biggest enclosed spaces.** To show just how big, 46 full-size hot-air balloons were inflated inside it in 1992! The record-breaking sunroof slides open to reveal open sky in about 20 minutes.

87 **Sydney Opera House was built twice.** The weird shapes of the Sydney Opera House roof were so far ahead of their time that builders had to start work before the materials for the roof had even been invented. When the builders realized that the roof would be heavier than expected, they had to blow up the foundations and start again!

88 **You can surf on a beach with a roof in Japan.** The Seagaia Ocean Dome is an artificial beach, with a sliding roof. Visitors can surf on artificial waves all year round. The building is 300 feet (100 meters) from the actual coast.

89 **In France there is a city of movie theaters.** Wonderful buildings are part of Futuroscope near Poitiers, France —a huge amusement park. Some of the theaters there have screens that surround the viewer, and one plays a 3D film on a screen that's 50 feet (15 meters) high and 65 feet (20 meters) wide.

▼ The movie screen inside Futuroscope's Kinemax building is the size of two tennis courts.

◄ The Sydney Opera House contains five theaters, 60 dressing rooms, four restaurants and six bars.

90 **It takes an army to run Disney World.** This amusement resort in Florida, United States, covers 146 square miles (120 square kilometers). It takes 45,000 guides, sales assistants, cleaners, cooks, medics, and other staff to keep the park running. Visitors buy nine billion burgers and seven billion hotdogs each year!

I DON'T BELIEVE IT!

The white cladding on the shells of the Sydney Opera House is built from one million ceramic tiles!

Reach for the sky!

91 **The tallest towers are twins.** The Petronas Towers in Kuala Lumpur are among the world's tallest buildings at 1,483 feet (452 meters) high. They were built for Malaysia's national oil company. There are 88 stories of offices, held up by 16 concrete pillars in each tower.

◄ The Petronas Towers are the tallest office buildings in the world.

92 **Some people have always built houses in the sky.** The Korowai people of Indonesia build their houses in the trees. Their treehouses, called *dobbos*, keep them away from the damp ground and out of trouble when the neighbors are unfriendly. Rope ladders are raised into the trees to keep enemies away.

93

You can rollercoast around one skyscraper. In the heart of the desert in the southwestern United States, the city of Las Vegas has become the USA's main city of entertainment. Huge hotels and leisure buildings are overlooked by the Stratosphere Tower. There is a rollercoaster that travels around the tower at the top, 985 feet (300 meters) above ground.

◄ The Big Shot and High Roller thrill rides travel around the top of the Stratosphere Tower.

94

Some skyscrapers dance in the wind. Very tall skyscrapers are pushed around by the wind, causing the top floors to sway. This can make people feel sick. Some skyscrapers, such as the Citicorp Center in New York, have weights at the top that are moved from side to side to make the building lean against the wind, cancelling out the effect.

95

The first skyscraper was built 120 years ago. Chicago was once built of wood, but most of it burned down in 1871. The old city was replaced with more modern buildings, including the ten-story Home Insurance building, which was the first to use a metal frame.

► Chicago's Home Insurance building used lighter steel beams to build higher and faster.

Space spectaculars

96 **Rockets are built inside the tallest room in the world.** Some space rockets are over 330 feet (100 meters) tall. As they are made standing upright, they need a huge building in which to be made. NASA's Vehicle Assembly Building (VAB) in Florida, United States, is a 525 feet (160 meters) high, with doors that are 456 (139 meters) tall—bigger than a football field!

97 **There are four main parts to a space shuttle.** Each part is designed to help with a certain part of the journey. The shuttle has its own engines, but also straps on a fuel tank and two booster rockets to help it into space.

◄ NASA moves shuttles from the VAB on crawlers – trucks that weigh 2,700 tons each.

98

The Hubble Telescope wears glasses. With shuttle trips, we can now repair broken satellites in space, or pick them up and bring them home for a service. The Hubble Telescope needed to be fitted with electronic glasses before it could begin sending home its amazing views of deep space.

99

You can stay in space for a year. The International Space Station (ISS) lets scientists stay in space for weeks at a time in a weightless laboratory. One astronaut stayed on board the old *Mir* space station for more than a year.

▼ The International Space Station runs on electricity provided by giant solar panels.

100

Human beings are amazing! The biggest wonder of the world is you— a human being. You can think and act in ways no other animal—and no computer—can. We may never meet anything quite as amazing as ourselves in the whole of the rest of the Universe.

I DON'T BELIEVE IT!

Astronaut John Glenn was 77 when he went into space in 1998. He first traveled to space in 1962, 36 years earlier.

Index